Pebble™

Desert Animals

Camels

by William John Ripple

Consulting Editor: Gail Saunders-Smith, PhD

Consultant: Michael A. Mares, PhD, Former Director,
Sam Noble Oklahoma Museum of Natural History
University of Oklahoma, Norman, Oklahoma

Capstone
press
Mankato, Minnesota

Pebble Books are published by Capstone Press,
151 Good Counsel Drive, P.O. Box 669, Mankato, Minnesota 56002.
www.capstonepress.com

1 2 3 4 5 6 10 09 08 07 06 05

Library of Congress Cataloging-in-Publication Data
Ripple, William John.
    Camels / by William John Ripple.
    p. cm.—(Desert animals)
    Includes bibliographical references (p. 23) and index.
    ISBN-13: 978-0-7368-3634-0 (hardcover)
    ISBN-10: 0-7368-3634-9 (hardcover)
    ISBN 13: 978-0-7368-9488-3 (softcover pbk.)
    ISBN 10: 0-7368-9488-8 (softcover pbk.)
    1. Camels—Juvenile literature. I. Title. II. Desert animals (Mankato, Minn.)
QL737.U54R55 2005
599.63′62—dc22   2004011164

Summary: Simple text and photographs introduce the habitat, appearance, and behavior of camels.

Note to Parents and Teachers

The Desert Animals set supports national science standards related to life science. This book describes and illustrates camels. The photographs support early readers in understanding the text. The repetition of words and phrases helps early readers learn new words. This book also introduces early readers to subject-specific vocabulary words, which are defined in the Glossary section. Early readers may need assistance to read some words and to use the Table of Contents, Glossary, Read More, Internet Sites, and Index sections of the book.

Table of Contents

4

What Are Camels?

Camels are big mammals with humps on their backs.

places where camels live

6

Where Camels Live

Most camels live
in deserts in Africa
and Asia. Deserts are
dry areas with few plants.

Body Parts

Camels have one
or two humps.
The humps store fat.
Camels use the fat
when they can't find food.

Camels have round feet. The shape of their feet keeps them from sinking into the sand.

Camels have
long eyelashes.
Eyelashes help keep
sand out of their eyes.

What Camels Do

Camels live in groups called herds.

Camels eat grass
and other plants.
Camels can go many days
without food or water.

Camels can carry
heavy loads. Some
camels carry people.

Camels walk across
the hot desert.

Glossary

desert—a dry area of land with few plants; deserts receive very little rain; many deserts are hot and sandy.

herd—a group of animals

hump—the rounded area on the back of a camel; camel humps are filled with fat; some camels have one hump; other camels have two humps.

load—something that is carried

mammal—a warm-blooded animal with hair or fur; female mammals feed milk to their young.

Read More

Jango-Cohen, Judith. *Camels*. Animals, Animals. New York: Benchmark Books, 2004.

Macken, JoAnn Early. *Camels*. Animals I See at the Zoo. Milwaukee: Weekly Reader Early Learning, 2002.

Internet Sites

FactHound offers a safe, fun way to find Internet sites related to this book. All of the sites on FactHound have been researched by our staff.

Here's how:

1. Visit *www.facthound.com*

2. Type in this special code **0736836349** for age-appropriate sites. Or enter a search word related to this book for a more general search.

3. Click on the **Fetch It** button.

FactHound will fetch the best sites for you!

Index

Word Count: 108
Grade: 1
Early-Intervention Level: 11

Editorial Credits
Mari C. Schuh, editor; Patrick D. Dentinger, set designer; Steve Meunier,
   photo researcher; Scott Thoms, photo editor

Photo Credits
Bruce Coleman Inc./Clem Haagner, 14; Joy Spurr, 10, 12; Leonard Lee Rue III, 4;
   Melinda Berge, 18
Corel, 16
Index Stock Imagery/IT STOCK INT'L, 20
Lynn Seldon, 6
Ron Kimball Stock, cover
Salem Al-Foraih, 8
Shaun Chan, 1